The Crosses We Shared

Finding Our Strength in Him

Patricia Stoiber Ott

Orange Hat Publishing
www.orangehatpublishing.com - Waukesha, WI

The Crosses We Shared: Finding Our Strength in Him
Copyrighted © 2019 Patricia Stoiber Ott
ISBN 978-1-64538-005-4
First Edition

The Crosses We Shared: Finding Our Strength in Him
by Patricia Stoiber Ott

For information, please contact:

Orange Hat Publishing
www.orangehatpublishing.com
Waukesha, WI

Cover image by Wojciech Kozielczyk via iStock

www.orangehatpublishing.com

This book is dedicated to my late husband, Robert W. Ott, in grateful appreciation for the love and support he always gave me.

The following story is based on true events in the life of Robert W. Ott. While the events are true - names, places, locales, events, and details may have been changed or modified to protect the anonymity of individuals.

Foreword

I am an average person. Born into an average family with decent parents and a nice brother and a sister, all three of us close in age. We had two younger sisters born at the end of the line who were disabled and non-communicative. We took care of them and loved them all the more. But it was difficult. This was the cross my family lived with and loved with. And we weren't perfect. But we never stopped loving each other.

We all have a cross to carry. They vary from person to person. Some people have one major cross. Others carry crosses that are replaced with bigger and bigger crosses. It's as if one tragedy builds up your strength so you can survive the next and the next.

How do you carry your cross? Do you resist and complain and drag that cross? That makes it more difficult to survive and impossible to be joyful. Do you pick up your cross and carry it boldly and with joy? That will develop character and inspire others. And can you help others carry their crosses while shouldering your own? This is what sets you apart. The only way to do this is to join forces with your Creator. When you look around and find yourself alone, you will find your strength in Him.

It's a journey we are on. To develop that strength takes both time and pain. No one gets through life without challenges. A well-lived life is one that overcomes challenges.

I didn't want my crosses. I became overwhelmed. I became despairing. And one day I looked in the mirror, and I was gone.

CHAPTER 1

Sometimes
We find love was in hidden places
Lost in the innocence of youth

Sometimes
The answer was there all along
Waiting patiently for the right time
The right circumstance

Usually
Love finds you when you are ready
When you have experienced enough
To welcome your prize

It was a cold day in December of 2004. I was sifting through the mail, finding the usual bills and advertising. There, between the water bill and the mortgage, was a letter. The writing was familiar but I couldn't place it at first. The return address brought the past back to me. It was from a very dear, old friend. I hadn't talked to her in over twenty-five years. I was delighted to find that her reason for writing was to reconnect.

I called her immediately and we talked for quite a bit. She said, "We've been trying to locate you for the last class reunion and nobody seemed to know what happened to you. I was hoping I would reach you!" She had a booklet from the reunion and asked if there was anyone I wanted her to look up. I don't know why exactly, but I immediately thought of him. And I responded, "Look Bob up and see what happened to him."

She did and offered his phone number. "Give him a call," she said. I did call, and his voice was unchanged from all those many years ago. Memories flooded me of happier times. He asked me, "So, are we divorced, or married?" I said with some embarrassment, "Divorced." And he replied that he was too. I could hear the smile in his voice. We talked for a couple hours and it seemed like we had never been apart.

We reminisced about our high school years. The time he walked me home from school, carrying my books. We were sixteen. Neither of us said much. We were both so shy. I remember he was tall, 6'1" to my 5'3". He didn't have a moustache back then. He was a big guy, clean cut and courteous. We walked for a little bit and suddenly he handed my books back and said, "Well, here's where I live." And he disappeared from the path, leaving me to walk the rest of the mile home by myself.

I remember about a year later we went to the baseball

game once, and even to dinner. But again, our shyness never got us past a few dates. The timing wasn't yet right and both of us moved on with our lives.

I had heard later that he had become paralyzed after a heart operation at the age of nineteen, and I felt sad for him. But I was already moving into my own life of misery. Our paths crossed a couple more times in the next few years, and each time we were like old friends, but it was fleeting. And then we lost each other for the next twenty-three years.

They were mixed years. Filled with happiness and much trauma. Physically and emotionally abused by my husband for years, I finally divorced, but I was left a shell of myself. I had little self-esteem left, but I managed to carry on day to day, simply struggling to stay sane. I was very unhappy. I felt very beat down and so alone.

CHAPTER 2

A sheep among wolves
...ready for slaughter

I think when I was young I got the wrong idea about life. I was a very fortunate young girl. I had a united family. There was no divorce, no violence. There were standards that had to be adhered to by my siblings and me. We knew where we stood with respect to behavior, and respect towards our parents and others. My large extended family was warm and loving, and I do think the world was different then.

The worst thing that happened at school was when someone got pregnant or got caught smoking in the bathrooms. For me, the world was safe and good and kind. Life was about love. We helped each other. We believed in God's goodness. When I was growing up we respected our elders. We were told parents, aunts, uncles, neighbors, and teachers deserved respect because they had lived longer and experienced more than we children had. I remember my dad saying, "Most people are good. There are a few here and there that aren't, but most people are well-meaning." And that's the criteria I judged my world from as a kid. And it's the criteria I judged the rest of the world by when I moved out of my parent's home and made my way into the world.

All too soon I found out that I was a very naïve person. I fell in 'love' with a young man very quickly, and before I knew it I was married at nineteen. What followed was an immature relationship that fell to pieces within months. Before the year was up, I found myself the object of physical abuse which I have come to find is the way immature people act when they can't get you to do what they want. Stunned by this abuse, and completely unable to process the how and why of it, I retreated into myself and found that avoidance worked for a while.

I remember a particularly stressful day at work when I kept rubbing my jaw because it hurt so badly. I assumed I had slept awkwardly and strained a muscle. I looked into the mirror in the ladies' room and saw bruising. Suddenly I remembered. I had been beaten the night before. I was astonished when I realized I had completely blocked it out.

It was during these years that I would hear about women who were abused and I remember remarking to a friend, "Why would anyone stay in an abusive relationship?" How strange that I didn't realize I was in one myself! Abuse is insidious. The abuser tells you the abuse is a result of something you said ("You never know when to shut up!") or something you did ("Why didn't you stop me? You knew what would happen!"). It is so easy to be drawn into a dance of abused and abuser. The world closes in and you are ashamed so you don't talk about it. In my unworldliness, I convinced myself that if I was more perfect as a wife, I would not be subject to the punishment that I received. Surely it was my own doing. So, the face I showed to others was happy. The life I talked about was good. But the reality certainly was not the fiction I presented. I managed to convince myself that it would be better if only I was better.

But he tired of me and left one day for someone else. And I tried to find love again five years later, having found another who I hoped would be the *one*.

I guess a person gets caught in a kind of pattern. I did not have God in my life during this time. The religion I had acquired as a child was still beneath the surface, but never really grew into anything. I was so intent on saving myself that I couldn't see that it wasn't possible alone. I married again to a man who I thought was protective, loving, and fun.

Within six months I was horrified to find I was in a worse spot than before. I had learned nothing. I had again been taken in by a smooth talker, this time with a hidden past. Seventeen years later, after learning that calming a violent person was safer than confronting one, I was basically a doormat. Initially I tried to stand up for myself and realized quickly that it only escalated the anger he had.

He'd go into fits of rage at a look or a wrong word spoken. Often the origin of his anger was impossible to discern. Yet I knew when he was provoked. His eyes would begin to blink rapidly, and his entire body would shake violently. Then the profanity, insults, and shaming toward me would ensue as he picked up whatever was handy and threw it at me. Broken furniture, broken windows, and my broken sense of self all demanded I do something different. He had threatened me if I left. I believed him and so I felt trapped. I said and did what was expected so that I would spare myself his response. I was scared to have an opinion. I was afraid to do something wrong. I was afraid of life. And then it occurred to me that all people don't live like this. I tried to escape, and the image I have to this day is that of a toilet plunger on my forehead. As I struggled to free myself of him, I would pull away and the plunger would pull me back. Over and over this happened and I was now so confused I might have qualified for what he always told me I was. "You're crazy!" he'd scream. "You need a psychiatrist! You are NUTS!" I got so confused I figured I was. And one day I summoned all my courage and I ran away from myself and from those who hurt me. I wanted to be alone. Even the divorce was a nightmare. But I had escaped and tried to start over again.

By now I was a damaged mess. I had become so afraid of men that I couldn't look at the men's clothing as I walked through the department stores. If a man talked to me I got nervous. I avoided speaking to men as much as I could. I found myself lowering my eyes in submissive acknowledgement of my inferiority when even passing by a man as I walked. There were certain products I couldn't buy because they reminded me of the men who hurt me for so long. Things like dish soap! I consciously bought anything but the brand my spouse had preferred. I gradually replaced everything in my home because each piece of furniture and even clothing brought such frightening memories that I had to dispose of them.

The damage done financially was catastrophic. It took six years to recover and get myself to the point where I had good credit, and began respecting myself again.

It was at this point, at the age of forty-nine, with so much baggage in tow, that I received that letter and made that call. I barely had a reflection or a shadow anymore, and no longer knew who I was meant to be. It was then that God placed Bob in my path and my journey back to life began.

He had been through a difficult marriage also and as we talked, we found so much in common. We decided to get together for lunch on Good Friday. We both had time off from work and so I drove the eighty miles to meet him where he still lived in our hometown. I sat and talked to him, face to face now. I noted the worn wheelchair that had been his legs for thirty years. He didn't look any different otherwise. He had much more confidence though! His smile was warm and welcoming. He listened intently to my story of abuse and then told me his. It was clear we were both very broken by our lives and somehow, we finally felt right at home with each other.

We went to dinner. I told him I'd buy since it was my idea to meet. We were just old friends getting together so I thought that would be right. He said, "Oh no. I don't want anyone thinking I'm unemployed!" We laughed about that as I watched him make the great effort of getting out of the car.

My experience with disabilities had begun when I was very young. Two of my younger sisters are profoundly disabled. But they are disabled in a different way. They do not communicate, cannot dress themselves or take care of themselves at all. They have been institutionalized since they were just a few years old. No, this was a different situation for me.

When Bob became disabled, it was due to a spinal stroke midway between the operating room and the recovery room. It left him paralyzed from mid chest down.

An interesting thing had occurred during the surgery. He died three times on the operating table, he was told. But what he remembers is incredible. He told me he remembers his surgery, at least part of it. He remembers floating above the operating table, kind of up in the corner. He could look down and see the surgery being performed on himself. He said he felt a great peacefulness overwhelm him. He was happier and felt better than anytime he could remember in his life. He would have been content to stay there, he said. Suddenly he felt whooshed back down into his body. The next thing he remembered was that he was in the recovery room. He told the nurses about his experience. They kind of laughed at him and said that couldn't have happened. He described the doctor that was operating – in great detail. They looked rather shocked, he told me, and said that was impossible because that doctor didn't come into the room until Bob was under anesthesia and had left before he was awake. How does one explain that? Since that time Bob was never afraid of death. He wasn't anxious to leave the world, but he wasn't afraid because he knew there was something wonderful beyond this world.

At that point it was discovered that he was unable to move his lower body. He had some feeling if his skin was touched, but he couldn't move. To top that, while still in his hospital bed, a minister told him the paralysis was because of a deep, dark sin he had committed! Bob ordered him to leave. Bob always believed in God, but due to that brief encounter with an uneducated religious man he became angry inside. So angry that he was inspired to prove a point. He would not feel sorry for himself, but busy himself with the idea of making his life over. I once told him that I wish we had married many years sooner and I felt we had missed so much happiness because of our late start. He replied, "I was different back then. Maybe you wouldn't have liked me much." It seemed this major life event had changed him in numerous ways.

After he had recovered from his surgery and was ready to move forward he'd gone back to school, got a degree in business and then in social work, and then took a job working with people with disabilities and teaching them what he already knew: That life was what you got and it was up to you to make what you could from it. No whining. Just perseverance. As Hubert Humphrey once said, *"Oh, my friend, it is not what they take from you that is important. It is what you do with what you have left."*

He touched others in a unique way. While working, he was able to inspire and direct clients with disabilities. His goal, after becoming disabled himself, was to find a way to make life worthwhile despite the disability. He wanted to show those with disabilities, through example, that life wasn't over. It was just different.

Over the years, through all his struggles with his disability and the health and lifestyle problems that came with it, he had developed an empathy for those who struggled like him and wanted to help them make their lives hopeful.

His family was a great help to him and he probably couldn't have done it without them. But his courage and his incredible stoic attitude is what made the difference. He could've rested back on disability benefits but he wanted to make a difference. He wanted a full life. He told me his goal was that people would see him no different than others and that once they got to know him, they would only see the man, not the chair.

He had great strength and courage. His mind was fine. He just couldn't walk. He had taken the challenge handed to him in November of his nineteenth year.

He went out with friends. He even went bowling! He had his own apartment, which he did his best to keep clean himself. He did his own laundry. He also had that nice little sports car which he used to get to work and back. He used a slide board which he would push beneath his upper thigh, with the other end on the seat of the car. Painstakingly, and slowly, he would do little hops and push himself along until he was seated in the car. Then he would fold up his chair and place it behind the seat. He had great upper body strength, mostly because in college he had played basketball on a traveling wheelchair basketball team, blazing the way for other disabled athletes at his college and earning many trophies. Wiggling himself into the proper position to drive, he used hand controls and drove his little red sports car with great delight. Driving was important to him. It was something he had control of! He loved to drive. In his car, no one could see his disability and he was like any other guy driving a sports car. That's why he never wanted a license plate that had a disability label. He used a hang tag for parking in handicapped parking spaces, but once he was moving again, no one would know.

My respect for him was immediate on that first day we met again. Over the next nearly twelve years I would always refer to this day as our first 'non-date.' He always referred to it as our first date. I was in no way planning to marry again. But he had already made up his mind.

We had a really nice dinner, complete with wine, and I was amazed at how being with him calmed me. He was a great listener. He was a counselor by occupation and he was as patient as could be. But he was also very reticent to do things and missed so much of life because of his physical limitations. By himself, he simply couldn't take certain risks. I, on the other hand, am a bit more daring. We complemented each other beautifully. As we began our new relationship, I was educated in a whole new world. I had always had respect and even sympathy for people who needed wheelchairs for mobility. But I never knew the full scope of how their lives were impacted.

Gradually, I learned how to size up a place for accessibility and ease of maneuvering, whether it was a restaurant, a movie theater, or basically any place he wanted to go. I soon learned that wheelchair friendly meant many different things to different people. We would laugh often at the outcomes of our little trips. Like the time he asked for the men's room and the clerk pointed up a flight of stairs to a 'wheelchair accessible' bathroom. It was an eye-opening experience to be in the world of disability. All the things people take for granted are a major feat for a wheelchair user; particularly a person who couldn't bear weight. Some people can get up, stand and move briefly to accomplish what they need to do, but Bob was completely unable to stand and that presented many challenges.

As I spent more time with Bob, I could feel myself healing. He had kind eyes and a smile that melted my heart. He made me feel beautiful and smart. It had been a long time since I had felt valued. I was no longer alone. WE began.

CHAPTER 3

The newness of love
Delighting in everything
Filled with anticipation
Soothed in acceptance
Radiating happiness
How long can it last?

We soon became inseparable. I was filled with joy at his genuine approval of me. I was really surprised to find I was interesting to him. He was respectful of me as a person first, as a woman next. I was drawn to him in fascination of his quiet integrity.

I had dealt with mental illness and meanness and I couldn't bear it. But this was different. His disability was not his personality. It was merely his paralysis. Oh, I don't mean to make light of that! His medical condition was questionable from the first date, but I was not daunted. He told me he knew he wouldn't survive past sixty. I wouldn't accept that. I had other ideas. I told him I'd take such good care of him that he'd be around longer than that!

We decided that we were 'meant to be', as his mother

put it. Within a year we got engaged and I put my house up for sale. We searched and searched, viewing about forty homes, to find a place that would work for him. Steps, narrow doorways, angles in hallways, and small bathrooms all were by-passed as being unsuitable to manage life in a wheelchair in. We considered building, but it was costly and neither of us made a lot of money. Finally, while trying very hard to find a place midway for both of our jobs and families, we had to concede that West Bend turned out to be the best we could do. We bought a home there in June of 2006 and were married in the backyard on a sunny day in July, just a week after his forty-ninth birthday. Bright yellow lilies provided the flowers in the background, Bob's choice of bluegrass music played from a CD player and his minister, whom he had known and socialized with for many years, pronounced the words that made us man and wife in the company of immediate family. Commentary by a couple of crows flying overhead at that moment predicated the future for us, as the minister was pooped on when they flew by. He didn't laugh, but the rest of us did.

So, I learned how he lived. The limitations he had were many. If it rained, we had to stay home. He couldn't chance getting sick because for a paraplegic it could mean pneumonia. Pneumonia, with his limited lung function, could mean death. If places were too crowded, he stayed away. He didn't like to be in the way, but he also didn't like following people in a crowd who might dangle a lit cigarette at the very height he happened to be at. Bob reminded me, with a sarcastic tone, of his view of the world in that position. I found it kind of funny, but his disgusted look said, "Not so much from my angle."

He had difficulty with restaurants because they were often very crowded. He felt he and his chair took up a lot of room and many times people would have to move chairs and open a pathway for him to get to a table. It embarrassed him and made him *feel* disabled. So fast food, eaten in the car, was the norm until we got the van many years later.

Going to a baseball game to see the young kids in our life play was also hard, because the fields were grass and sometimes muddy. Not a good place for a wheelchair to be! Rarely was there a field that had a sidewalk or concrete, which made it much easier to get to. The sun was also an issue. Paralysis for him meant he sweat just sitting there. The sun made him sweat more. It taxed his kidneys, which were prone to infections and sweat created skin breakdowns, which led to pressure sores. There were so many things that the world did not realize. He wasn't just sitting down, as he liked people to think. He bravely faced his many challenges without complaint.

Immediately his caregiver became me, although he did many things himself for the first couple years, I helped him a little by washing him and helping him get dressed. I took time each evening to attend to his feet. He had some terrible sores that wouldn't heal, and after two years I was proud to say they were gone. He had refused to go to a doctor, claiming that the doctor would amputate. I also did wound care daily to a chronic sore on his hip. Several years earlier, before we reconnected, he had an infection in his pelvic bones which doctors could not seem to cure. As it was chronic, there was a drainage site. Bob instructed me on the care of the wound and I took over from his paid caregivers in this and in catheter changes. He knew what had to be done and was patient and brave in being subjected to a novice doing it.

At this time, he was capable of getting in and out of bed using his slide board and washing his own hair. He loved to make breakfast and made a mighty fine omelet with toast and coffee for us in the mornings before getting himself into his car and going to work. He was home before me since my drive was the long one (1 hour) and so he busied himself folding clothes and doing dishes before I got home. We had installed an awesome electric lift in the garage when we bought the house. This made his disability private. Too often we saw houses with wooden ramps built to the front door, signaling a person with a disability lived there. Not only did that bother his pride, it was advertising that we were somewhat compromised in defending ourselves to some who might take advantage of that.

We shared making dinner responsibilities. On the weekends we tried to get out and do something enjoyable. Life was good for us both. We were in a rhythm and we got along so pleasantly.

I knew he hadn't been many places since his paralysis and that he had missed a lot. I found what he enjoyed and made every attempt to fill in the missing parts of Bob's life. We enjoyed Civil War re-enactments, historical sites such as the Springfield Lincoln Museum and Galena, Illinois. We went to wine tastings, out to dinner, took drives in the country, and went to movies and plays. We laughed and talked and healed together from the hurts both our lives had dealt us.

We made plans to go to Gettysburg and a Dude ranch in Arizona. Those things, however, were never realized. We had waited too long because after three years his health began to deteriorate at an alarming rate.

It began with a kidney infection and hospitalization. When he returned from the hospital I got him up in his chair before going to my work. When I got home I saw his chair through the bathroom door, which was ajar. It was empty. In panic, I called to him. He said, "I'm in here. I'm on the floor." I said, "Well, what are you doing down there!" He had reached over, lost balance and slid out of his chair. As he landed, his right leg twisted and became pinned underneath him. He managed to crawl on the carpet about halfway into the next room, thanks to the tremendous upper body strength he still had for those first few years. I was going to call an ambulance to make sure he was ok. But, because he had little feeling in his lower body, he said he thought he was fine. The worst of it, he told me, is that Lucy re-runs played on TV for the four hours he lay there. He never liked that show! The paramedics came because I couldn't pick him up off the floor. He was a big guy, about 260 pounds at that time. They took him in at my insistence because Bob said he heard a kind of crackle when he landed. At the emergency room he went into shock and suddenly they were scrambling to save his life. X-rays showed a break in his thigh and in his lower leg.

Weeks of hospitalization followed. A break for some people would be bad enough. But Bob was borderline diabetic and had high blood pressure. Paralysis complicated things further because his circulation was terrible and any pressure to his skin would cause skin breakdown. He spent 3 weeks in the hospital with a gigantic cast, lined with layers and layers of padding to prevent pressure. It would be changed every few days at first and then each week and x-rayed to make sure no damage was being done to his skin and that the bone was actually healing. Meanwhile we were advised that he was in kidney failure and that it could be controlled for a while but it would not improve.

Once home, our life never was the same. He eventually went back to work for bit. He and I designed, and I sewed, a special pocket into the seam of each pair of his pants.

The pocket had a hidden zipper to match the color of the pants. The purpose was to put the leg bag into that pocket. Normally the catheter led to the leg bag which was kept attached to his upper calf, behind the knee, with a strong elastic band. As his skin was starting to break down there too, the new invention was meant to take pressure off the skin. It worked beautifully and every hospital and nursing home he was in after that would be impressed with our invention. We made a good team! Bob went back to work after a few more weeks, but the leg took about a year to heal.

CHAPTER 4

Love is a choice
In the face of my love I saw the suffering face of
Christ Our Lord
There is where my strength lie
I could do all things needed through Christ
It was He who strengthened me

"Whatsoever you do for the least of my brothers,
you do unto me."
– Matthew 25:40-45

We'd been married close to four years when the wound disaster struck. Memorial Day weekend of 2010 was a typical holiday. My dad had just left from his annual month-long visit with us. I was doing Bob's personal cares for the morning which included a bed bath. As I turned him over to wash his backside I noticed an area that had a dark tinge to it. It looked a little tender so I washed it gently, but the second I applied the washcloth to it a grey fluid spewed upwards like a geyser. In a panic I grabbed towels and paper towels to soak up the fluids. This was unfamiliar territory and I didn't know what I was dealing with.

I bandaged him and took him to the hospital. There, they didn't even know how to get him from wheelchair to exam table. They apparently were not used to dealing with paraplegics there. We were told they couldn't do anything about the problem and gave us information on a wound care doctor he would have to see after the holiday weekend was over.

This began the wound problem he carried the rest of his life. We saw various doctors, none of them knew how to fix this. I assisted at a surgery in the office of one wound care surgeon as she cut away black, dead tissue. The surgeon decided to debride the wound in her office and had no assistant so she asked if I was willing to assist her. I watched as she nicked a blood vessel that bled profusely. I handed her instruments and sopped up the bleeding. I watched her with her knife as she cut into his flesh, exposing healthier tissue beneath. Good thing I had a strong stomach for all this. It was stressful to be a part of but I could handle it because I had to if I was to be of any help to Bob.

I was instructed in wound care techniques which I performed twice each day. Trips to the wound care clinic were often weekly, sometimes (when the wound looked a little better) we were able to put off a visit for a couple weeks and even a month. Various remedies were tried over and over to no avail. Tests revealed a chronic bone infection still under way and we were told it could not be fixed, just held at bay until it would take over and end his life. In order to get him to these appointments I had to get early appointments, when possible, and then make up the time I'd lost at work by going in earlier and working through lunches for the rest of the week. For seven years I took most of my vacation time for doctors, hospitals, tests, etc., in order to get Bob the help he needed to stay alive. I was always exhausted from lack of sleep, overwork and too much stress. Trying to maintain a light attitude and enjoy life so Bob would also be happy was sometimes very difficult.

It was during this time of our marriage that I was truly tested. Consumed by worry, work and caring for him I found myself despairing. I had come so far in happiness only to be given this huge challenge. I would feel sorry for myself on many occasions. Others had no comprehension and little knowledge of what our life had become. There was wonderful support by several people closest to us, but most people just had no idea. Some things cannot be understood unless, as my mother would put it, "They have walked in your shoes." And I desperately tried to handle it without bothering anyone.

Thinking I could do all this by myself was a grave mistake. My health started to decline, both mentally and physically. But I had no time or money left to address these things. My focus HAD to be on Bob as he was in such terrible condition. Nothing going on with me could compare to the pain and suffering he had during these years. After that crisis was past the next years brought more and more problems with his health. His skin had broken down on his backside after the hospital got the chronic hip sore to heal. He told them not to heal it because it was necessary to drain the hip infection. But they knew better and healed it up. But it only healed on the surface. Bob was always convinced that the draining found its way out a different route and that is what caused the new sore to form. This sore, treated for the next seven and a half years, would never heal and would ultimately be one of the causes of his death in 2017.

Hospitals, nursing homes, and rehabilitation centers followed. For a couple years he spent half the time at home and half the time away. Eventually he wore out his leave on his job and lost that. Losing his job was like losing his identity and sent him into a major depression. He loved his work. It gave him meaning. He became very unhappy. Losing his job also made me the sole breadwinner and caregiver for someone who was becoming more and more bedridden. For a time, I was completely on my own. I tried to talk to him about finances and he told me I had to deal with all of it because he couldn't stand thinking about it. He didn't even want to hear about it. He told me I had to be the strong one. I couldn't talk about the bills with him. Or anything else. I handled mountains of medical bills.

With that came insurance issues. It was nearly a second job to follow up with the problems from incorrect billing and insurance processing.

Chapter 5

Buddy

When Bob first became confined to his bed for more hours than not, he was lonely and depressed. I had to be gone for long hours each day in order to work to support us, and I wondered how to provide some comfort for him while I was away. I suggested finding volunteers who could visit with him and he wasn't interested in that. I did the next best (and as it turned out, the very BEST thing) and got him a living, breathing companion to share his lonely days with.

I had suggested we get a dog a long time ago, but Bob was insistent that it would be just that much more work for me. He knew and appreciated the strain I was under and didn't want to make it worse. I had dropped the idea for a time. As he was less and less able to get out, the idea of a dog kept gnawing at the back of my mind. Just on a whim then, one day driving home from work, as I passed the Humane Society I found myself turning into the lot. As I walked through and looked at all the animals who had no home, I found myself liking the idea of getting Bob a dog more and more. I walked by the big dogs which

I knew Bob would really love. It would be difficult for me to take care of a big dog and make sure he got enough exercise. As I walked by some smaller dogs, one dog in particular caught my eye. He lay there in the oversized cage looking about as pitiful as could be. As I passed by he made no sound except a little whimper and looked back over his shoulder at me just like one of those TV ads and won my heart. His big brown eyes looked soulful. He knew. I knew. It had to be him.

He is a Jack Russell Terrier / Chihuahua mix. He is the best dog ever! His name was Pipsqueak. I had to wait a few weeks to claim him since he had to be neutered. He also had a kennel cough that needed to be eliminated. I went to see him each week while I waited. Finally, one day, I got the call that he could be picked up and taken home. I wrote a note, complete with a photo of him. I wrote the note from Pipsqueak to Bob. The next morning I left the note underneath Bob's coaster on his side table, knowing he wouldn't discover it during the day. The note pretty much told Bob that Pipsqueak needed a home desperately and would he please, please let him live with us and just love him?

I picked the dog up that night and returned home. I stopped in the driveway and made a call to Bob. I asked him to please read the note beneath the coaster. And I waited. All of a sudden, I heard Bob say, "You haven't left him in the garage all day, have you!" I reassured him that the dog was with me and I had just picked him up. I asked if he was mad at me for going over his head and doing this when he told me not to. I asked him if I could bring him in. Bob just said, "Let me see him."

The moment Bob laid eyes on his new dog his heart melted. I saw the biggest smile on his face as he asked, "Is he really mine?" I explained the waiting and the visiting and assured him he was his very own companion for when I was away. He said, "I wondered why you kept coming home late so often." I told him to name the dog. And Pipsqueak became Buddy because every time Bob would call him, he automatically called him his little buddy.

It took little time before Buddy was spending his days mostly on Bob's bed. I would come home often to find Buddy curled up on Bob's pillow. Bob, stretched out on his stomach would have his arms circling around Buddy. Bob's head lay on Buddy's back. I was so happy. Bob was in heaven! In that hospital room which used to be our bedroom, with its hospital bed and alternating air mattress to help prevent bedsores Buddy was working on Bob's morale.

We would take Buddy with us when taking our little rides, but usually he was just at home with Bob. That was his job. We took Buddy with us to his nephew's house for a birthday party for one of the kids about three weeks after we got him. Buddy loved other dogs and small children, and was getting along well when suddenly he went into a terrible seizure. Fortunately, our niece is a veterinarian and diagnosed his epilepsy on the spot. I guess that's why he was given up then. But we couldn't do that. I took Buddy to our veterinarian and she prescribed medication to be given twice a day. It didn't eliminate the seizures, but it did make them a rare occurrence. Buddy needed us and Bob needed Buddy. Surely another *meant to be* moment.

We had to purchase a Hoyer patient lift. We had low carpeting, which made moving it a little easier. But a job that was a two-person job in the hospitals or nursing homes became a one-person job for me. My age, combined with the carpeting and sharp angles I had to move him at in the lift, soon tore the cartilage in one of my knees and I had to have surgery to repair it. He was stuck in bed for about a week, as there was no one who could get him up for us. On crutches, I did all the usual cares for him and he patiently waited until I could get him out of bed again.

The Hoyer lift that I used to lift Bob out of bed with became a toy for Buddy and a source of entertainment for all of us. As I lifted Bob up into the air in the sling, Buddy would leap up onto Bob's lap and take the ride to the wheelchair with him. Other times, when Bob was in the chair, Buddy would crawl as best he could up the side of Bob's chair, looking to be petted. It was little moments like these that made us smile and eased our burden.

We needed help to handle everything but it seemed impossible to find the kind of help we needed and could afford. We prayed together every day. We gave thanks for what we had and asked for help for what we needed. We prayed more earnestly during the hospital stays. We would pray together out loud before I left his hospital bedside each day. On more than one occasion an aide or nurse would come into the room, realize we were in prayer and smile sweetly at us.

CHAPTER 6

The more you try to hide
The more gleeful the devil is
Finding your weakness
Enjoying your pain

And I lost myself amid the sounds and the smells of the casino. Within its crowds of gamblers who neither knew nor cared about me, there was no judgment. Here I was alone, but not. Here I leave my problems outside and find solace in nothingness.

BONUS! Immersed in the lights and the sounds of the slots I sat for hours, just shoveling money into the slot. Hoping for a win, but really not as concerned with that as with the escape I found. Sometimes I won, but mostly I lost. I lost if for no other reason than I bet higher and higher and played longer and longer. Even if I did win, I would play until I lost it all again. Why would someone like me do that? I had so much responsibility both at work and at home. I controlled the budget, watched how much I drank (couldn't be drunk when you are always the driver, and when a paralyzed person depended on you twenty-four hours a day). I controlled everything in my life and most of my husband's life. All depended on me. If I was sick or hurt my household fell apart. I HAD to always be strong. Perhaps that is why I could find a release here. When Bob was in the hospital and very sick I'd sometimes go to the casino after seeing him to release the tension that was getting worse and worse within me.

It started with a couple hours to unwind, but soon the evil that lurks in the casino just as the evil that lurks in alcohol or drugs, began to rapidly work on my mind. And I spent more time and more money there. I also found I could stay all night, not sleeping or eating or drinking anything to hydrate my body. Going without basic needs pretty much labeled me a person with a gambling problem.

So that's what stress can do. People say stress is harmful. It certainly was to me.

Some days, while caring for Bob, I would become so frustrated I would excuse myself, run into the next room and close the door. There I would take a moment to sob convulsively to relieve the pressure of my emotions. It was there I begged God to help me in genuine fear that I could not manage any further. Then, comforted by His presence, I would take a deep breath and go back, smiling and joking with Bob. But Bob knew how hard it was. He knew me too well for me to hide it. I know it hurt him that it was so difficult for me. And I added that to my list of worries because I just couldn't be as good a wife as I wanted to be. I felt like I was failing him.

I hated giving him injections. It made me so nervous, but I did it. Middle of the night bed changes were made often when his bladder was failing. Worse still were the bouts with intestinal illnesses. I had to change the bed with him in it, which was difficult. Then in the middle of the night I would be running loads of wash to clean the soiled, wet sheets and blankets. Going to work with four hours of sleep or less left me angry and frustrated at times, despite my determination to do what needed to be done with joy.

I wasn't perfect in my caregiving. I tried very hard, but resentment at the loss of my own life began to nag at me. I worked, I did personal and wound cares. His room had become a hospital and the closet a pharmacy. It was overwhelming. But I saw such goodness in Bob. He was so patient. How could I possibly fail him when he was the one suffering? I had the easy part, but it didn't always feel that way. I became ashamed of my weakness in dealing with it all.

He seemed to be going nowhere in his healing. We consulted a different doctor for a better opinion. He at least tried to help by putting Bob into the hospital and using incredible amount of antibiotics over six weeks to try and kill the infection in his pelvic bones, which is where this draining had tunneled from. The doctor told us at that time he had a 60% chance of survival. But it was better than nothing.

The gaping open wound didn't heal. More hospitals, more surgeries, always with complications of pneumonia and kidney infections. When the flap surgery was performed and Bob became despondent from weeks on his stomach and hallucinations from medications, that's when the gambling became a problem. He was on oxygen and as I sat next to his bed watching him breathe through his mask, his eyes suddenly opened very wide and he screamed, "Fire drill!" I called the doctor in immediately. He listened to the gibberish Bob was speaking and decided to do a brain scan. It was eventually decided he had an allergic reaction of some kind to the anti-depressants they had given him. We would often laugh about that incident later, because it was so bizarre.

Staff had me bring his childhood teddy bear, the blanket that I had made him and anything else that he would find comfort in, because he was so despondent.

Eventually he was moved to a rehab unit. Ultimately, he came home. And this scene repeated itself several times in the coming years. So often, in fact, that they blur together in my memory and I have trouble now remembering which hospital he was in at any given time. I can recount five hospitals, three long term care intermediate hospitals and four nursing/rehab centers. He was in several of them multiple times. He was usually in the hospital, in intermediate care and in rehab successively before coming home from most of his hospital events.

Nearly six months after having gone in for this particular surgery he was finally coming back home and I found myself in the casino again. Terrified at the additional care he required from me. I was lost because I had no one to help me cope. There was no one to turn to. There was only me.

Overwhelmed at the medical costs that were edging towards $500,000 for this event alone, I stared at the slot machine in a daze, pushing the button...just pushing the button until I put the last dollar I had on me into the slot. I was startled out of my thoughts when I heard a voice say, "That's ENOUGH!" I jumped a bit and looked around. Then I realized it was my own inner voice. Who was that? Was it my conscience? Was it God? Were they the same?

I stood and slowly walked over to the security desk and I said, "I need you to ban me from this place." They photographed me and took my information down. They said I would be banned for one year and if I were to be found in their casino during that time I would be arrested and escorted out. If I ever wanted to return, I would have to submit a formal letter requesting re-admittance.

I went straight to Bob to tell him what I had done. I explained my problem to him. He knew I'd been to the casino but he no idea how deeply I was troubled. He was very supportive and kind to me. Finally, he was out of his own apathy because he was now worried about me. He even told me he was proud of me for recognizing my problem and for banning myself. But he said, "There are other casinos though. What's to prevent you from going to those? You need counseling." And he was right. I looked up Gambler's Anonymous and began going to meetings there. I found there are a lot of people who have this problem. Like any addiction, its base is rooted in emotional issues, not in the addictive behavior itself. I needed to figure out why I could not control this. Gambler's Anonymous is an organization begun by the Franciscan priests of the Catholic faith, I discovered. The meetings began in prayer, then confessions of each person just like in the movies which began, "My name is Pat Ott and I have a gambling problem." And then an explanation of how you were out of control and how it was affecting your life and the lives of those around you.

I listened to various people talk about the issues of their lives and how they were driven into gambling by their own inadequacies and weakness. They talked of losing jobs, families and friends and of legal issues arising out of their problem. We worked through the step program of finding forgiveness to offer to others affected by our weakness and ultimately to forgiving ourselves and finding strength through one another to support a new way of coping. We always ended in prayer. I was proud to get my first token of sobriety after 30 days, another after 90 days. I stopped going after that because I felt I had a handle on it.

I had gone back to my Catholic roots, attending Mass

weekly and for a while even daily. I went to confession and prayed for strength. My first few Masses I found myself crying without control because I realized that I had been trying to fill an emptiness with a vice, when it should have been filled with Faith in God.

To please Bob and to show him my dedication to our marriage I was able to quit gambling just like that and would not return to it again except for 1 time several years later when I told Bob I wanted to see if I could try and be in control. He nodded approval. I took only what I felt I could afford to lose and when that was gone I came home and told him I couldn't go back. The same urge was still there and it was difficult to break away from it.

Bob and I started talking about God a lot. He began to read and study his Bible every morning. I began reading the Bible and attending religious day retreats, reading Catholic books and trying to understand what was missing in my life and how to cope with what my circumstances were. I began taking Communion to elderly in nursing homes, volunteering in small ways at church, sewing and donating blankets to homeless people. I prayed and prayed and prayed for healing.

Bob was supposed to spend only two hours sitting each day. This was so limiting that literally he should have stayed in bed all the time since it took one and a half hours for me to do his wound cares, wash his body and his hair, dress him and get him up into his chair using the Hoyer lift. By the last couple years he was unable to do much of anything himself.

My return to Faith came at the right time because I was more and more pushed to my emotional and physical limits by caring for him. I tried very hard not to show emotion when dealing with the less pleasant aspects of caring for someone so terribly disabled. Because he had to lay on his stomach to heal the wound on the back, he developed another wound on his knee. The wounds were awful, both in look and in smell. I spent most of my time either working or taking care of Bob. Volunteer work that I managed to squeeze in became my therapy. My yard that was once filled with flowers and kept with great care began to see neglect and it was all I could do to keep the house clean and get Bob to all his appointments. I tried to visit my children and their families as I was able and between it all I was getting more and more exhausted.

One of the hospitalizations Bob had was very lengthy as a plastic surgeon tried a skin flap to help heal the wound. Bob was told to lie flat on his stomach, without any movement, for three weeks. While there, aides turning him accidentally pulled out the drain hose. It was not replaced and soon he had another infection. He was so despondent that he was given medication. The medication was heavy and again it made him delusional. He had such a difficult time with being 'trapped' for so long.

All kinds of treatments, therapies and medications were

tried. He'd get better, then worse. He'd come home for a few months and suddenly have another kidney infection to send him back.

He got very ill one day and called me home from work. I saw the fever in his eyes. His temp was 102 degrees, his blood pressure was very low and he was dry heaving. I rushed him to the hospital in a very familiar routine. He slumped in his chair as I drove. We got there, according to doctors, just a half hour before it would've been too late. He was admitted to a room and in an hour or so he couldn't breathe. He was rushed to intensive care and intubated. He had sepsis. His breathing worsened.

Doctors and nurses told me not to get my hopes up. He was a very sick man. He was like that for about ten days. I brought in a minister, the same one who married us, to pray over him. A friend from my church and his sister Kathi joined me in prayer over him. We cried because it didn't look like he was going to survive.

I prayed in my car that evening after leaving the hospital. I remember telling God that whatever his will was I would understand. I asked him to heal Bob and if he did I would never stop loving or caring for him my whole life. But if it was time for him to go home to God, then, "Your will be done," I said. But I added, "Please, please don't let him suffer. He has suffered so much already."

I was at the hospital most of the time, on vacation from work. I went home briefly to sleep. My sleep now was worse than ever. I got a retainer because I kept waking up grinding my teeth due to stress. I developed terrible acid reflux. One night during this illness of sepsis I had a dream. Although she had died years earlier, I heard my mother's voice, "Patty, WAKE UP. WAKE UP!" And I jolted awake, finding myself choking violently due to acid reflux. I had been so dead asleep that I couldn't wake up to my body's signals. I'll always wonder...

The doctors decided to try and bring Bob out of the induced coma of the intubation. His other signs were better and it looked like they had gotten the infection under control. But how his lungs were now was the real issue. I coached him as he came up out of the coma, reminding him to breathe and listening for signs from the machine that he wasn't getting enough oxygen. The nurses were called in many times to correct his breathing. It was terrible for him and for me as well.

Although he came out of the intubation, his doctors still cautioned us that he was not out of the woods. His lungs were badly damaged and did not hold oxygen as they should. Bob was given two choices. Re-intubate and scope his lungs to look for the cause, or try steroids. Steroid treatment was not really a good option, we were told. Rarely, although occasionally, steroids were found to open the airways and correct the problem. But it usually didn't work, and had the extra effect of making blood sugars very unstable. If he survived he would experience threatening issues with his diabetes. Intubation had been very difficult for Bob and he wasn't anxious to repeat it. Bob did not hesitate, and he did not look worried. He looked at the doctor and simply said, "Steroids." And that was that. And they worked.

While all the focus was on Bob's lungs and infection, the wound had been deteriorating. Bob was on a huge air mattress which shifted pressure constantly. But he had been on his back during this whole time. The wound had been ignored. Their priority had been getting him to breathe on his own again.

I asked the doctors to turn him over and see what the wound looked like. There was a group of specialists there at the time and when they turned Bob over and the wound was revealed, my reaction was one of horror. And the doctors said nothing in front of Bob, but the look on their faces told the story. One doctor muttered, "I'm so sorry," under his breath as he walked by me. He looked at me with pity and sadness. The wound looked ten times the size as before and was very deep. It was also completely black. Lack of oxygen from his breathing problem and the infection itself had ruined all the healing he'd been working on for years. I asked for the wound doctor and was told, "No surgeon will touch him in the condition he's in." My reply was, "And you know he will die from it if no one tries. They have to try." A wound doctor was brought in. Carefully, she cut away the black every day, as much as was safe to do. His diabetes did indeed become much worse and his blood sugars dangerously fluctuated.

But, eventually he was stable and the wound showed slow signs of improvement. He was moved from his ten-day ICU stay into a room on the third floor. Four days later he was off to a nursing home to recuperate for three months.

He came home at the end of the year. It was December 28, 2014. Nurses were sent to our home to monitor his breathing and his wound. After a few weeks Bob told them not to come. He told me he felt safer in my care and so we went back to our own routines and were happy he was home again.

Chapter 7

"Compassion is not seeing someone's pain.
Compassion is sharing someone's pain."
– Unknown

As a young girl, I asked my mother once when a person was finished. What I meant was, at what point is a person fully aware of who they are and have they then reached their full potential as a human being? Mom answered, "Not until you die, honey. You are always changing and growing until you die.

I have had a lot of time for reflection in recent years. There was a time when I thought I was a pretty good person, made a lot of right choices, and that I was perhaps better than those around me. Ouch! How filled with pride I had become. Sometimes you grow in virtue, but apparently sometimes you first grow in fault. It often takes a major life event, or a series of them to understand what path you are taking.

Hopefully, you find out soon enough to turn it all around and do things better. I believe people are all on a journey back to God. I believe life is to learn how to love

God and others more perfectly. And I know in my heart that God is with us every step of the way to lean on when we stumble and to direct us to the light, if we have faith.

I've always wondered why bad things happen to good people. I was raised to think that if you did the right things, good things would happen. Cause and effect. Maybe that's why I was constantly amazed, all my life to see that terrible things happened to many good people. And I wondered why. Matthew Kelly wrote:

"Deny yourself, Jesus was clear. He didn't promise or even allude to an easy path. He did not promise comfort. He promised quite the opposite. He set denial of self as a primary condition of discipleship, and He promised that each of us would have a cross of our own to carry."

To care only about oneself is not discipleship. We have to help each other through our lives.

My friend, Brad was a devoted husband and father. His wife had just given birth to their third child.

Another friend, Al, was about to retire a little earlier than he had expected to. He had been quietly battling his own terrible disease. Al and Brad were very good friends.

It was Al who had first told me of Brad's wife's stroke. He and I had many discussions over the years about God and Catholicism. He and his wife, whom he referred to as, "his beloved bride," were staunch Catholics. Al asked me once how I managed with Bob. How hard it must be, he mused. "Where do you get your strength?" he asked me.

He told me that people in crisis are either drawn closer to God or push themselves away from Him when facing major events such as Bob's unrelenting illness.

Then he took me aside and told me what few people were aware of at the time. He told me about Anna's stroke. He said, "I needed to tell you because I know you will pray for her." I was honored at that trust. I prayed very hard for her daily. My Rosary was the weapon I used against her devastating stroke. And many others in their church and at work, family and friends, were also praying for her.

Al and Brad and I exchanged e-mails often with encouraging words and support. And then she recovered! Not completely, as to this day she has difficulty with speech and comprehension a bit. But miraculously she is well enough to go forward.

Al's disease paralyzed his vocal cords and he could no longer speak.

Then, just as Brad's wife was recovering from her stroke, Brad was diagnosed with another challenge. And there I was, somehow having gotten mixed in with their battles too.

I was stopped by him as I walked past his home one evening.

"Pat," he called nervously. I stopped and walked back to where he stood by his door and looked at him quizzically. "Yes," I answered. He said, "Will you pray for me?" And, of course I said I would. I was a little confused because we had been praying for each other for a long time already. He suddenly blurted out that he had just received a call from his doctor telling him he had a brain tumor. His wife was getting ready to take him directly to the hospital. I was shocked. I remember mumbling that he would be ok and not to worry. I hugged him and went on my way feeling very powerless to help and frightened for him and his family.

He had brain surgery within two days to remove a large portion of the tumor but it wound itself in and around his brain and no more surgery would be beneficial. He had chemotherapy and radiation. Quickly his condition degraded so that he had double vision, couldn't make sense with his words, and felt paranoid and sick all the time. Yet he continued to pray for Bob. He continued to communicate with me and to pray for me. Bob and I prayed for him and his family too.

I was paged at work one day and when I answered the page, it was Brad. Speaking in an almost unfamiliar voice due to his illness, he said that he desperately needed a hug. "Everyone is afraid to touch me," he said. "Will you hug me?" He asked me to meet him downstairs at the back door so no one else would bother him. I went downstairs to meet him. His mother was at the wheel of the car. As I looked in to talk to Brad, I saw the bucket in the front seat. He was coming back from another round of chemotherapy and radiation. He opened the car door and stood up very unsteadily. I wrapped my arms around him and stood there holding him for several minutes. His mother smiled at me and nodded as I said, "When my daughter was little and she was sick, I would do this for her. I am hugging my strength into you." He was so weak and childlike. This man had been one of the healthiest and most successful persons I knew. Yet this illness had leveled the field and somehow, here I was taking care of one who was the boss over many others. Titles mean nothing. Money means nothing. Kindness and compassion are what matters.

When he was admitted to hospice four months after his diagnosis, his wife asked me if I could use our wheelchair van to get them to their church on Sundays. I came from fifty miles away to pick them up and drive them to their church and then back. One day he and I waited in the lobby for his wife to join us for the trip to the church. As he sat there in his wheelchair, propped up, tied in so he wouldn't fall over, so very weakened by his illness, I saw tears quietly slide down the sides of his face. I looked into his eyes and I could see the extreme sadness and futility there. I got a Kleenex and gently wiped his tears away as he was too feeble to even lift his hands himself. As I looked into his eyes I said, "This is very hard, isn't it?" And all he could do is nod his head and cry a bit more. I felt his pain. I related his pain to Bob and knew in my heart I would face this again someday soon.

It was during one of these visits that I found a little

time to be alone with him. I said to him, "Brad, I need to talk to you about something." He had been silent and lost in thought, but looked up at me from his wheelchair and asked, "What?" And I explained to him how important his friendship had been to me. I told him I had known a lot of unkind men in my life and that he was different. "You are one of the good guys," I told him. And then I said, "I love you like a brother, Brad. That's the kind of love I have for you." And his eyes misted over and he looked so sadly at me as he said quietly, "And that's the kind of love I have for you too." Dying people need to know their lives mattered. And Brad mattered.

I visited him frequently, sometimes bringing our other friends along and encouraging them not to abandon him because he really needed them now. The visits were short because he often just stared straight ahead and was incoherent. But in between these events he knew us and was glad we were there.

One of our friends who also visited often told me she went to see him one day and he expressed happiness that lots of people came to see him. He was so glad people cared. She asked, "Brad, who comes to see you?" She smiled as she told me his response. "Pat comes to see me!" he said. And I was so happy my visits seemed to help him.

His sister-in-law asked me to come over just before Valentine's Day and take her, Brad, and his father to a store so he could buy a last gift for his wife before he died. I remember teaching his father how to maneuver the wheelchair in and out of the van and how to get through the store. His chair was oversized and we had to be careful not to bump Brad, who was very weak by now. His medical equipment hung on the side of the chair and we needed to be careful not to wrench it from him. They all cried when he found the perfect gift because it was truly the last loving thing he could do for his wife whom he loved so much.

We had a curious connection. One day, his wife asked me if Bob could come to see him. At this time Bob was doing poorly, having had a blood clot diagnosed in his leg. He had been told by the doctor not to move more than necessary. But Bob's concern was not for himself, but for Brad. Brad needed some emotional help in coping with being trapped in his body. His wife Anna said Bob was the only one they knew who would understand and be able to talk with Brad.

Bob and Brad spent an hour behind closed doors, discussing what they needed to talk about. Anna said it helped calm Brad. I think Bob's days as counselor were important here and I could see he felt glad he was able to be of help.

A hospice was really the last place I thought Bob would go into. I'm sure that it was a scary reminder of what Bob was facing. In fact, when Brad died shortly after that visit in February of 2016, it would be almost exactly a year later that Bob would face his own death.

I became a "Prayer Warrior" for these men and for Bob. I prayed my Rosary for all of them and I prayed Chaplet of the Divine Mercy specifically for Al at his request. He went to the chapel at church at the 3:00 hour on Fridays to pray and he was so grateful that I prayed this for him too. He prayed for us and for Brad. We all prayed together for strength. None of us was alone.

I keep in touch with Al through email. And I have come to know his wife as well. They still refer to me as their "Prayer Warrior".

The last time I took Brad and his wife to church we left services early because Brad was anxious and not doing well. As I drove back to hospice with his chair locked down next to me in Bob's spot, he complained of being too hot. He picked at the seatbelt that kept him in place and somehow managed to unbuckle it. I reached across and held the chair in place with my arm because I wasn't in a place where I could stop to fix it.

I drove those last few miles very nervously, afraid Brad would die as I drove. His wife, Anna, was in the back seat and I don't think she was aware of what I was working with.

Once we got back to hospice, I silently breathed a sigh of relief as the nurses took him back to his room. I nervously asked Anna if he was ok, all the while realizing what a dumb question that was because we all knew he was dying. But she didn't want me to feel bad and she bravely patted my arm and nodded, "Yes, he is fine." That was the last time I saw him. He died three days later.

I was asked by the family to do his eulogy. Me. A person afraid of crowds and especially public speaking. But it seemed important to them so I wrote my speech. And when the time came, I walked up to the stage in the Bible church, past Brad's coffin, and stood at the podium. With microphone in hand, my voice sounded out over the crowd of about 200 people as I told them about my friend.

I was surprised to find many people told me I did a great job. I know the strength did not come from me. It was possibly the first time in my life that I was able to speak in public without fear and anxiety. All of that left me as I walked towards the microphone and I was calm and confident, without shedding a tear, in front of all those people. I needed to do him justice. Experiences are never your own. Somewhere, someone has already suffered as you are and it is easy for none of us.

Chapter 8

Shortly after Bob's recovery from sepsis he had another kidney infection, which led to yet another hospitalization. He also had his bladder stop functioning and went through a very dangerous twelve-hour surgery to remove his prostate and bladder. He was stapled closed and given an ostomy to expel urine. I watched him carefully for signs of infection. The doctor told me he had a rough time doing the surgery on him due to his other problems and would be surprised if the foot-long incision in his belly didn't "split wide open and his guts spill out." I was nervous caring for him then! He said if that happened, I should shove them back in and call an ambulance. Talk about stress! All the while I was being educated in ostomy care, while still doing wound care, etc., etc., etc.

And he healed from that too. He was one tough man. His courage during all this was amazing. He was gentle and kind. We kept each other going. That is, until he just got too tired to go on.

His sixtieth birthday was in July of 2016. I kept remembering what he had said when we met. "I won't live to be sixty." And I kept thinking, "You will!" I talked to his sister Kathi, and together with his family we planned a surprise birthday party. I put together a memory book for him. He was always rather sad that he felt his life had no meaning and wondered what good he was, just being there in bed and always so sick. Kathi provided many photos of his entire life and I asked his friends and former co-workers for anecdotes and photos they could share.

I worked on the memory book during my lunch hours at work. With my boss's permission, I scanned the photos into the copier and emailed them to my computer. There I would take and organize photos and stories and build a memory of his life. I had it on my flash drive and once it was completed, I had it printed at a local print shop. There it was, for all to see, the story of Bob's life.

The party was wonderful. Held in his sister's back yard, there was room for many people on that beautiful happy day. Friends and relatives gathered to celebrate his life with him. He was filled with smiles and it was apparent that he was very happy. There was a ton of food and a beautiful bakery cake with decorations. The cake also included a photo on an edible image. It was a silly high school memory and made him laugh. Kids played, adults talked and reminisced. It was a wonderful way to celebrate the life of someone who had been pretty much shut away for years because he was so ill. I told Kathi I wanted to celebrate his life while he was still with us so he could know how many lives he had touched.

And then one day he said, "I'm getting so tired of this,

Patty. I don't know how much longer I can do this."

Within a few months another problem had surfaced. The doctors claimed it was gout, then carpal tunnel. I don't think they really ever got that right. From October on he had tremendous pain in his right arm. It was continuous and unyielding. No medication seemed to help it. At that same time, I noticed he did not communicate during the days anymore.

In past, he would text me occasionally at lunchtime, checking in to see how my day was and to tell me he loved me. I rarely got a text anymore. When I asked him about it, he said he was sleeping. He was incredibly tired, he said. But he also slept all night. He said he was bored lying in bed all the time. He was in pain and it made him tired. He had so many excuses. I'd come home from work and talk to him and he'd fall asleep while I was talking. I teased him, "Oh, am I boring you? You keep falling asleep!" He'd just say he was so tired. Even when he tried to talk to me while I was looking at him, he'd trail off as he spoke and fall asleep, apparently boring himself as well.

I knew in my heart that he was dying. His wound, although healed somewhat again, wasn't able to heal completely. Other complications included very inconsistent blood sugars and constant chronic pain. His quality of life was at an all-time low and he was confined to his bed most of the day. All signs showed him on a down-hill slide.

He had been told by a young doctor several years earlier that there was nothing they could do for him and that he would eventually die of the wound. This caused us so much pain, and I remember Bob and I both crying in the doctor's office as he sentenced the rest of our lives together without any emotion at all.

When he was feeling good, I'd try to get him out a little for quality of life. Although we were told by the wound doctors that he shouldn't sit up more than two hours a day, I pointed out that we couldn't even go to the doctor with that time frame. Quality of life won out over and Bob's decision was to have something to look forward to.

We did short trips. We'd take a drive, go for dinner somewhere local, always watching the clock and trying not to be overdue. If he got tired, we'd stop what we were doing and rush home to get him to bed quickly. When he got tired, he slumped in his chair and there was the worry that he would slide out again or that his wound would get worse.

The wound got better and worse. Our favorite doctor, whom he saw during the seven years of trying to heal, was a great guy. I asked him privately once if the wound would ever heal. He hesitated, but then said he never wanted to stop giving his patients hope. He admitted though that it would never heal. I promised not to tell Bob. But when this doctor changed jobs in the fall of 2016, a new doctor took his place who believed in being frank. He told us flat out that the wound would never heal and that I should take Bob home, take care of it myself and enjoy what was left of his life.

After his party and as fall approached, with his new issues of gout, carpal tunnel, and his falling asleep I knew his days were coming to a close. With the new wound doctor losing all hope, Bob said he just wanted to live a little. We went to a musical in Green Lake and that was so much fun. I took him on a train ride to Chicago and back and he was so happy. But hope was gone. And without it, Bob declined very rapidly.

Surgery for the supposed carpal tunnel was scheduled for January and then postponed a week. Bob seemed relieved it was changed. I said to him, "I thought you wanted relief from your hand and arm pain." He said he was dreading this surgery. "Something feels different this time," he said. "I don't think I'm coming out of this one. If anything happens and I can't communicate, I want you to bring me the blanket you made for me and my dog, Buddy." I scoffed at him, inwardly frightened but trying to make things lighter. I said, "It's only an arm surgery, Bob. You'll be just fine!" But people know when their time has come. And Bob knew too.

We were all set to go, waiting for the surgeon. The doctor came into the room and announced that the surgery was cancelled. Bob's white count was through the roof. He had not had blood work done before the surgery, even though it was ordered. We tried several times but Bob's tiny, deep veins would not yield to a blood draw and after numerous attempts each time, the technicians would give up. We decided we'd just get it at the hospital before surgery then, because they would be hooking up an IV anyway.

They told us to go home and make an appointment at the clinic to see what was wrong. I objected and asked if they couldn't just get him a room, because he never got anything simple and wouldn't it make more sense to run their tests and get an IV going right away? The nurse seemed surprised at the logic of this and agreed. Bob got a room and IV's were started immediately. They diagnosed another kidney infection.

Two days later Bob was on oxygen. Two months later, he would die of COPD, pneumonia, sepsis, and complications of diabetes.

CHAPTER 9

And the day comes when nothing can stop it
His will is done

When the operation was cancelled and the subsequent failing of all his systems was finally upon us. We stood firm in love of each other and of God.

In mid-January, from his hospital bed, Bob looked at me and said, "I've asked God not to take me yet because I don't want to leave you all alone." Stricken, I could do no more than look at the ground.

He then said, "Don't worry, I have Jesus with me." I was stunned at his calm. We had not yet been told he was dying but he clearly already knew.

In those next two months he suffered so much. I tried so hard to comfort him. One doctor I am still angry with was a lung specialist. He came in to see Bob while I was there. He looked at Bob, who was on a C-Pap machine with an oxygen mask, and told him he was fat and that he would die. He explained as if to a child how Bob should be eating little bits like he tells his little son to do. He said Bob had COPD because he had a fat neck and a fat body. He was horrible and I was stunned into silence, seething and afraid to say anything for fear I would beat him bloody. I watched Bob lay there, wordless and I could see tears streaming down the side of his face through his oxygen mask.

When the doctor left, I'm afraid I did cause a scene and demanded a different doctor. I told Bob how upset I was and he said he was waiting for me to blow! I kind of wished I would have blown up at that doctor. I guess I missed that opportunity. But the next doctor and the nurse heard about it!

Test after test, medication after medication, but nothing proved helpful as Bob's lungs deteriorated. Soon they moved him to the intermediate care hospital. Day after day I tried to visit before work, go to work, go back to help him eat at noon, come back to work, and then go back after work trying desperately to keep my job and not leave him alone.

Yet his blood sugars began to fluctuate wildly, his lung machine constantly sounded alarms and his general condition plummeted. I spent several nights in the chair by his bedside, afraid to leave him. The doctors then told us to make final plans because he had little time left.

Bob was always worried about me. He knew the toll all these things were taking on me. In the days before he was to go into the hospital that last time, he sent me an email at work.

"1Peter 4:12-13 Dear friends, do not be surprised at the fiery ordeal that has come on you to test you, as though something strange were happening to you. But rejoice in as much as you participate in the suffering of Christ, so that you may be overjoyed when his glory is revealed. Trials, so often, seek to bring out the worst in us. Many times they succeed, and we quickly become dangerous to those closest to us. It is as if thieves are trying to steal away all the fruit of the spirit from within us." Galatians 5:22-23 says, "But the Holy Spirit produces this kind of fruit in our lives: love, joy, peace, patience, kindness, goodness, faithfulness, gentleness, and self-control."

"When trials come to you, it is an opportunity to depend upon the sufficiency of Jesus Christ more, and more, and more, and more. Rejoice, not because the trials are punishing you, but because you are being led towards deeper relations with God, and a more complete understanding of His grace. Living for Jesus means sharing in His sufferings and letting Him be your refuge and strength."

We listened as his kind doctor carefully spoke to us about Bob's prognosis. He told Bob he would not get better and that it was time to think about final things. He was somewhat vague, letting it settle in softly I suppose. It's a lot to handle. After he left, Bob lay quietly just looking ahead. We said nothing at first. Then Bob said, "Well, I guess we need to talk about a few things. Cremation I suppose. St. Mary's Cemetery." I gently corrected him, "Holy Angels, honey. We belong to Holy Angels." He responded, "Oh." After a moment or two he started to talk about what he wanted to do when he came home. I told him I thought about putting a fence in the yard so Buddy could run. And we didn't talk about *it* again.

Within a week he would develop pneumonia in both lungs. He was no longer breathing on his own but with a bi-pap machine that breathed both in and out for him. I had spent several days there due to his worsening breathing. His appetite was very poor. His vital signs were too. And after another terrible breathing incident, he was considered stable so I went home to sleep.

No sooner had I walked in the door than the hospital called saying they were transferring him to an acute care hospital because his breathing was worse again and they weren't able to turn it around this time. His oxygen was dropping lower and lower. I drove the fifty minutes back, this time a little further to the emergency room of the hospital they were moving him to.

I was taken to the emergency room where I was told by the charge nurse that he was in respiratory failure. They were pumping oxygen into him through that mask and it was making the most horrible sounds. I told them to give him something for anxiety because although he showed no emotion on his face, I knew his eyes and they were terrified. I remember saying glibly, "For God's sake, give him something for anxiety. And while you're at it give me something too!" I was hysterical at that point and crying. The nurses were trying to find a vein for an IV and I was upset because again I had to watch them stabbing and stabbing at his poor worn out veins. I hated to see him hurt. Bob looked at me through his mask. He reached up with his good arm and, staring into my eyes he cradled my head lovingly with his big hand and he said, "Don't look. Don't worry. I'm ok."

The emergency room doctor asked Bob about a tracheostomy, which was his only chance at survival. He had been asked that once before and had responded, "NO! I'd rather die." His response at this moment was a violent shaking of his head and a loud "NO!" again.

Settled into his room in intensive care later, he was sedated and relaxed, breathing evenly now. I went home for the night to sleep and hurried back the next day.

His nephew and niece and their spouses visited him. His best friend made a final trip to see him too, despite his own very precarious health. I'm so glad they could see him one last time. I know it must have been very difficult for them to see him in this condition. But at least they saw him awake, because by the next day he no longer was.

Doctors tried to drain his lungs to help with the pneumonia, but they were solid. Each thing they told us was another disaster. As I sat with him that day among the many tubes and machines, I watched the oxygen monitor anxiously. Suddenly I saw the numbers start to fall. They continued to slowly go down and I wondered why no one was coming in.

Finally, I went out and asked at the desk, "Why isn't anyone coming?" The nurse came into the room and quietly said, "There isn't anything we can adjust. The machine is on maximum settings." The nurse looked at Bob intently, then looked at all the machines. He suddenly reached past my shoulder and smacked a button on the wall. Instantly a camera came on with a live doctor and there were people everywhere. Bob looked at me and quietly said, "They are going to intubate." And that is the last thing he ever said to me.

The doctors asked me lots of questions about the strength of his heart and his other conditions. They asked me if I knew his last wishes about being kept on a machine. I responded strongly and without hesitation as I knew his condition better than my own. One doctor said, "That's what I need to know. You really know what he wants, don't you? And I said very sadly, "Yes, I do."

I wanted to leave quickly so they could get him taken care of. I hated to see him struggling and in pain. One doctor said to me, "Say good-bye." And I stopped, looked into Bob's mask and simply said, "I love you." I don't remember seeing him. All I saw was that mask. I left his side so he could be intubated.

The doctor came to talk to me in the waiting room. He

told me that Bob had told the doctor at the other hospital what he wanted but had done so when I wasn't there. I guess he knew I couldn't handle any more. Bob had told the doctor that if they intubated him again to wait for a few days and if there was no improvement to let him go.

This matches what he said to me around that time during one of his breathing episodes. As he struggled for breath, he said to me, "If they intubate me, don't let it be forever."

The next day, Sunday, I gathered together the book I made for his sixtieth birthday party, along with my Bible, and went to visit him. As he lay there peacefully unconscious, the machine breathing audibly for him, I spoke to him. I told him all the things I wanted to say the week before but simply couldn't bear to say because that would make this all too real. I read all the nice things people had written about his life from the book and I read his favorite Psalm from the Bible. I told him he was the best thing that ever happened to me and that I would carry him forever in my heart. I said, "You have fought so hard and have been so very strong and courageous. But it is time to rest. I know your mind is still very strong but your body just isn't able to survive any more. It's time to go home to God." A nurse came in to check on him as I finished speaking and suddenly Bob's hand, which I had been holding, gave me a strong squeeze and I exclaimed, "He heard everything I said to him!" She smiled and nodded at me.

A little later, his male nurse from the first night he was there came on duty. He came into the room to check Bob's sedation and tubing, etc. He needed to make an adjustment as Bob was restless, coming out of the sedation briefly, kind of choking on the tube for an instant, which frightened me. The nurse needed an extra hand and so he asked me to hold some tubes so he could make adjustments. I was pleased that I could do yet one more thing to make Bob more comfortable and as I held the tubes connected to Bob for the nurse to work with, I was rather surprised to find my hands very steady with no shaking at all. And I felt humbled to be able to help him.

The doctor asked me to authorize a do not resuscitate order for him. After discussion and understanding exactly where we now were, I agreed. Then the doctor said, "I saved his life by intubating. That's my job. Now you have to decide how long to keep him on the machine." He said Bob had no hope of recovery.

I told him I would tell him the next day. I needed time to think. I saw Bob and was so relieved that he was unconscious and looked at peace. No more struggling to breathe. I went home to try and sleep a little.

It was early evening and before I could try to rest I called my Priest to help me decide the moral and ethical way to manage this decision. We spoke for a while and he was very helpful and assured me that letting Bob go was appropriate in this situation where there was nothing further that could be done. It would be letting nature take its course and I felt somewhat better. I didn't want to be responsible for his death.

I was to go to the hospital the next morning by 8:30 or so and meet with the team of doctors to determine how long to keep him on the machine. I was letting the dog out before I left and pacing nervously in the side yard, praying and crying and begging the Lord to make this decision. I prayed it was not my decision to make, it was God's and please, please, don't put this on me!

As I was driving to the hospital about half into the drive, I got a call from the hospital that Bob's blood pressure was dropping. I said, "I'll be right there. I'm on my way."

Not ten minutes later, and I remember exactly where I was on Hwy 164 in Sussex, I suddenly felt a strange, gentle kind of wash across my heart. I had a sudden sense of peace and I said to myself, "No need to hurry. He has already passed."

But as I reached the hospital, my step quickened and I nearly ran into ICU. As I approached his room I gradually slowed because three nurses were standing at the door waiting for me. Of course, I knew he had died. They hugged me and assured me he had not died alone. His time of death seems to correspond with that wash across my heart. And I remembered what I had told him, "I will carry you forever in my heart."

I looked at my dear husband laying there. The machines

were still breathing for him as he had died only ten or fifteen minutes earlier. As I stood there memorizing his face and stroking his hair and hands, the doctor came in to pronounce time of death. And our good God had spared us both. He took Bob home to be at peace, no longer bound by his forty-year paralysis and continual illness and pain. He spared me by making the decision only His and I am forever grateful for that.

I took care of the arrangements by myself. I planned a nice funeral with a lunch. I invited my priest, because I am Catholic, and his pastor, because he was Lutheran, so we had it all covered. I bought a tombstone with both of our names on it so eventually we would rest together forever. I spoke at the funeral, having written a eulogy to try and express how important Bob's life was. "Please don't forget him," I implored them.

And because it was February, and still winter, I had to wait to bury the crematory urn which stayed in my living room until Good Friday. Then I had him buried in Holy Angels Cemetery next to a veteran of WWII who had earned a purple heart for valor. I knew Bob would like that. As promised to his mother, his teddy bear was buried with him. Good Friday, the anniversary of our first 'date' eleven years earlier.

I was stoic. I was strong. I got everything practical accomplished. I could handle anything. And when I cried, I cried alone.

And, I thought I had conquered my gambling addiction. But after he died I was back in the casino within two weeks.

CHAPTER 10

"Carve your name on hearts, not tombstones.
A legacy is etched into the minds of others and the
stories they share about you."
— Shannon L. Alder

This is not the end of Bob's story, but the beginning. He worried he would not be remembered. He will never be forgotten.

Bob lives on in the hearts of many lives he touched throughout his sixty years of life. He had many good friends he still kept contact with from his childhood. I, of course, can only relate what I know from my life with him.

He was joyful and friendly and had a reputation as a warm and steady kind of guy. He claimed he had all kinds of women who looked to him as a brother over the years. Everyone seemed drawn to share their troubles with him. He was calm and thoughtful. He always spoke only after giving a lot of thought to the question. He always said, "I don't want to offend." He was careful like that. He never wanted to hurt anyone.

He rarely ever raised his voice. I remember one time a telemarketer called and was quite persistent. Bob was trying hard to get rid of him without being mean. Finally, I heard him say goodbye and hang up the phone. He said, "Man, I just feel so bad having to yell at him like that." I laughed and said, "I didn't know you were yelling! Is that the best you can do?" I had been screamed at and criticized and sworn at so much in my previous twenty years that I couldn't believe my good fortune that this was as bad as it could get with him! And it proved to be the truth because over the eleven years we were together I can't think of a time when he did anything more than scowl when annoyed. He was safe to be with!

After the first three years of our married life, when the medical problems began in earnest, there were many opportunities to see his effect on others. With his elderly mother he was calm and patient. I was impressed at his gentleness with her as her dementia progressed. While in hospitals and nursing homes (so many I've lost count) he drew people to him in the same calming way.

There would be aides and nurses visiting him first to do his cares and then to linger to talk to him about their own problems because he was soothing and so very kind. He was patient there too. Sometimes the call light was on for half an hour and no one came because of how busy they were. Yet he was never mean once they did. He always thanked people who helped him. He always thanked me for helping him too. People began to refer to him as Saint Bob on some of those hospital stays. I was proud to be his wife.

I remember when he said to me one day, "What good am I, just laying here? I can't do anything. I can't help anyone. I feel so useless."

I remember saying to him that he was spreading God's love by comforting the many people he met during his continuous medical events. Because he spread kindness, compassion, joy, and hope to those he met, he also evangelized the word of God everywhere he went. Through our trials together both of us had been brought closer to God. And we were not afraid to express that. And we developed a reputation for being the 'angel couple'. That was pretty awesome!

CHAPTER 11

Nothing can stop God's plan for your life."
– Isaiah 14:27

I had taken care of all the millions of details that need to be addressed when a spouse dies. I had methodically and logically gone through the processes. People kept telling me how strong I was. I simply dealt with it without emotion. I'm sure it was important for me to keep organized, so I would feel I wasn't losing my mind. I had prepared for this mentally for years. Yet here it was and it truly wasn't anything I was prepared for after all.

The best sign I had that I was hurting was my lack of sleep. I normally can fall asleep easily, usually from exhaustion. The times I slept poorly were the times Bob was in intensive care and I was so incredibly worried.

Now it was all over, the stress suddenly gone. And yet at night I would wake up four or five times a night. At first, I would lay there feeling relaxed. Then the memory of Bob in the last days would cause me to grieve without warning. I cringed at the visual picture of him in my mind, yet tried so hard to remember so I wouldn't forget what he looked like. I strained to remember his voice. I was so afraid it was gone forever.

Sometimes I would dream about the hospital and all that had occurred and wake up terrified, only to realize it was history. Bob didn't suffer any longer.

The funeral had been on Friday and I went back to work on Monday. I had been so touched that about twenty people I work with had made the fifty-mile trip from Oconomowoc to West Bend to support me at the funeral. As I stood and greeted the people who came through the door, I was happy to see friends of Bob and of mine, family, and even his wound care nurse. But what shocked me was seeing my first co-worker, and then the rest all followed. Such a beautiful support system!

Bob's mother sat quietly on a chair at the front of the room, next to Bob's picture and the urn of his ashes. His teddy bear that was eventually buried with him sat leaning up against his photo. The teddy bear was the first toy he was given when his mom and dad adopted him at the age of six months so long ago. He had always treasured it. She talked with Bob softly as she sat there. It was a difficult day for her and the rest of his family who gathered together this last time for him.

So back to work, beginning my life over again. Within a couple months I decided to sell the wheelchair van. It wasn't necessary anymore and cost a lot to repair, operate and insure.

I'd never sold a car before so I googled it. Found out what I needed to do and placed an ad. I cleaned it up really good, gathered all the paperwork together, invested $400 in brake repair and then gave it an oil change. I waited.

Meanwhile, my friend Al emailed me that he was in a terrible dilemma. His wife had fallen and broken her leg and now needed transport to the doctor. Because she was in a wheelchair and her leg was in an extension cast, she had to travel by ambulance or transport van like mine. Their budget was really stretched due to his illness and now this! He wrote that the first thing that popped into his head was, "Their friend Pat." And he asked if I would be able to help them. Of course, I said yes and arranged with my boss to do like I did with Bob. I would take the time in the morning for them and made up the time lost from work for the next few days. Their appointment was in ten days.

That same evening, I received a call. An elderly gentleman needed the van for his wife. She was currently in rehab and would be returning home in a week. He needed transportation as she was not doing well and he said he wanted to give her one last nice summer before she died.

He took it for a test drive and said he had checked me out completely and determined I was honest. He even called the place I got my car repairs and maintenance done at to ask about me. He had looked for a while and couldn't find a decent van he could afford. Everyone wanted a lot of money for a van that was in questionable shape, he said. And then he found my ad and he said it was a gift from God.

I had been told I should try and get $7,000 for the van I had paid $45,000 for it only four years earlier. Wheelchair vans owe half their cost to the conversion needed to make them wheelchair accessible. I still owed $3,000 on it and had just purchased a different car. I did my homework also and was told by a mechanic that I could get between $7,000 and $12,000 for it. A friend told me to shoot for $13,000 and so I did. My new friend John said he would not argue the price because he needed it and he felt it was a fair price. He was happy I had kept it in good repair and it also looked very nice.

He put money down the same night. And said, "When can I pick it up?" I explained my promise to my friends and he understood completely. He made me promise to be very careful. "Don't have an accident, now. I NEED this van!" I told him I would have to put another 150 miles on it before he'd have it for his own and he agreed. He would pick it up the evening after I helped Al and Sara.

Meanwhile, he asked if I could spare some time to instruct him in the use of the van if he brought his wife's wheelchair over one evening. I spent a couple hours showing him how to maneuver the chair in and out safely and lock it down. He was so nervous and afraid he wouldn't remember how to do it. He didn't want to chance hurting his wife. I explained it and showed him and then watched and guided him as he went through the motions of it himself until he felt confident. We got to know each other during this time. It turns out he was a Vietnam war veteran and knew my priest.

The day arrived for Sara's doctor appointment. I felt it appropriate that the old van would make that one last trip to help a disabled person. Sara rode in Bob's place, just as Brad had done, and I felt an odd twist in my heart as I took her to and from her appointment, with Al sitting in the back as Anna had done on the rides to church with Brad. They were very grateful but I doubt they realized the significance of this last ride for me. I actually felt sad late that day when John gave me a cashier's check for the balance due on the van. I filled out the receipt and handed it to him. He said, "This is the nicest experience I've ever had buying a vehicle!" I then presented him with a get-well card for his wife and one of the prayer blankets I made to comfort her and keep her warm once fall weather made travel less comfortable. He was so pleased. We hugged and parted friends. He called me when he got home to let me know the van worked well and he made it! And his dear wife wrote me a thank you note a week later. It felt good to be useful. I don't think I will ever be the same since Bob died.

I felt so lost. My purpose was gone. I had been rejected so much in my life and now had lost my soul mate too. What was I supposed to do now? I decided that I felt good when I could do something to alleviate the pain and suffering of others. In reaching out to others I found validity. I knew what it was to feel overwhelmed and alone.

I began to look for opportunities to increase my volunteering. I had been doing some things for years, but I felt now it was my mission. What else did I have left? I try to honor Bob and glorify God in the ways I can to help others who are lonely and on the fringes. People that are overwhelmed by suffering and need a little help in the form of a smile, a gesture of some kind of caring. And I find they are all around me.

The suffering of this world takes many forms. I reached out and found people reaching back. They were filled with gratitude at the smallest offer of kindness. I am often surprised at how much I notice now. Are there more people suffering like this, or has being in the middle of so much suffering finally opened my eyes?

I had found my purpose. I was finding joy in life by serving others and as time went on, I was surprised to find I received much more than I gave. Selfishly, it made me want to do more. I finally was recognizing what I was meant to do. The person I was meant to be. And I found peace in serving God through serving his people. I have now realized that God loves me as the unique person I am. "Since you are precious and honored in my sight, and because I love you." (Isaiah 43:2)

And that gambling problem, which had begun again after Bob's death and continued intermittently throughout the entire next year, one day completely came to rest because it interfered with my volunteer work. The money, the wasted time, the devastating effect on my mind and body were suddenly not anything I could justify no matter how I looked at it. And I simply stopped again. And this time, I am confident there is absolutely no reason to go back. I have decided to replace vice with virtue. I have found myself. I am worthy. I have value.

And I am glad I have a gambling problem. You probably wonder why.

CHAPTER 12

*"Truly, truly, I tell you, unless a kernel of wheat falls
to the ground and dies, it remains only a seed; but if
it dies, it bears much fruit. Whoever loves his life
will lose it, but whoever hates his life in this
world will keep it for eternal life."*
– John 12:24-25

Years ago, when my mom died, my sister Karen told
me she had said, "Continue the legacy." What did she
mean?

We were going through her personal papers and I was
struck by the content of everything I read. Things she had
written, newspaper clippings she had kept for many years,
poetry and photographs, all had a main theme. She was
consumed with the idea of service to others and being
kind. What a beautiful legacy to continue! In the years
since her death I have thought about this a lot. I wondered
in what way that was to be accomplished.

Coincidentally, immediately after my mother's death I
noticed an increase in my prayer life. My long hour drive
to work each day became filled with thoughts of her and

I found myself praying more. As I drove I would begin to pray my Rosary more and more and became obsessed with singing the beautiful hymn "On Eagle's Wings", the words catching in my throat and making me cry when I came to the words, "Make you to shine like the sun and hold you in the palm of His hands."

As I went through this day after day, week after week in the time following Mom's death, I also noticed a change in the way I internalized my prayer. The words used to be just words. Now, as I prayed, I developed a new style of prayer for me. I placed pictures of the person I was praying for in my head. The result was that I felt closer to that person. I could tell it meant much more because I would cry as I prayed for the people in my life. And along with that realization came another.

As I prayed to God, I could see Jesus and his mother Mary in my mind but they were very far off. As I continued my daily prayers, over time the images seemed to move closer and closer to me. It has been years of this kind of praying and now when I pray, I feel Mary is next to me and Jesus is right inside my heart. Right there where I told Bob I would carry him for the rest of my life.

I began to realize that our close relationships with the Saints in Heaven and with Jesus should be at *least* as close as the relationships we have to those we love on earth. Because life is eternal. Because love never dies. And now, instead of feeling empty because of those I have lost due to indifference or death, I feel a certain comfort in knowing I am not alone.

But why is my flaw a good one? Because it is a reminder that I am not perfect. It is a gift of humility. I had not gone to a casino for many years and thought I had progressed in character so much! Yet I realized now I had been deluding myself due to pride. I thought I could control it and that, of course, makes me more perfect. What I didn't realize was that having a flaw and acknowledging that it was part of me was beneficial. I am reminded of The Lord's Prayer. The phrase, "and lead us not into temptation," is significant. God is in control, not me. My flaw would always be there and I was not meant to control it, but to find a way to live with it by avoiding temptation. I needed to lean on God's strength and accept my flaw in order to become a better person.

No one is perfect except God. Satan and the fallen angels made that mistake in the beginning. By feeling they were equal to God they doomed themselves for eternity.

My flaw and recognition of my littleness in comparison to God can save my soul. I know now that all I can do is recognize I have a weakness and look to God's strength to use that in a way that will help others.

I've always been told I try too hard. And I guess I always have. That can be damaging in relationships. But if used in the correct way, like anything else, great things can be accomplished.

Like what I was able to do for Bob. Trying too hard was necessary. And I will use that obsessiveness to help others have better lives. It gives me joy, purpose and a feeling of goodness that I cannot get in a casino.

With this knowledge comes peace and the realization that I must keep trying to better myself. Because God has created me out of love for love. Knowing I am loved by Him gives me the confidence I need to go forward, and serve.

CHAPTER 13

"Do small things, with great love."
— St. Theresa

When Bob died, I made a promise to God. I prayed, "I will dedicate myself to serving you for the rest of my life." It seems fitting to give back by serving God's people in whatever way I can, in order that I can continue the legacies of both Mom and Bob. Each does God's work, according to his unique gifts. So, what gifts do I have that can be used for the good of others?

First, I have Buddy. For several years before Bob's death, during all those illnesses, Buddy made frequent trips to hospitals and rehab/nursing centers. He followed Bob wherever he was, giving Bob that little bit of something extra he needed to keep going. I had to get special permission and Buddy always behaved very well. Despite the equipment and smells of these places, Buddy showed no fear of these things and was very delightful with the staff and other visitors. When Bob got sick, he would ask me to bring Buddy. Buddy would sit on the hospital bed with him and Bob would smile.

When Bob and I visited his mother in each of the two nursing homes she would be in, Buddy came along for that too. He trotted smartly down the halls just looking for people to notice him.

Usually the halls were lined with wheelchairs. The faces of the elderly would light up at seeing Buddy. They would reach out to pet him and most often a dialogue would ensue. The dog was a great ice-breaker. I heard stories of their own pets they had loved over the years. Sometimes the stories would be accompanied by wistful comments about how she or he had owned a dog but had to put it up for adoption when they entered the nursing home. Oh! How they missed their pets.

It seemed appropriate, when looking for my gifts and talents to give to others to remember that Buddy had proven gifts and talents also. Buddy had been lost when Bob didn't come home. Each day I'd drive home and when I took Buddy outside he would stop and try to see into the van to see if Bob was there. He seemed to mourn his loss and it was very touching.

I have gotten Buddy certified as an official Therapy Dog. During his assessment it was clear that is what makes him happy. Lots of love. He can't get enough petting! For his certification, we had to be assessed as a team by a certified assessor for the Therapy Dog Association in order for them to register him and provide insurance. The assessor was impressed with Buddy immediately and we visited patient after patient at the nursing home and hospice she worked at for two visits, visiting roughly fourteen patients.

He was comfortable enough to go up to a wheelchair and climb up the side immediately looking for his pets from someone he had never met before. The assessor was very pleased. He let people pet him, tug on his ears and he enjoyed it all. Our last assessment was my choice and I choose my sisters' home.

My two younger sisters, in their fifties, live in a group home with two other developmentally disabled adults. I wanted Buddy to be able to visit there as well and bring my sisters and their roommates the same kind of joy Buddy had given Bob. The visit went very well. My sisters have quick movements due to cerebral palsy. A roommate will suddenly shriek with laughter and make lots of noise. None of it bothered Buddy at all and so he passed his inspections with flying colors and the assessor made note on the application that we were, "A good team!"

Bob would be so happy to know Buddy continues to provide 'love therapy' to many others. He learned how to love from Bob.

Chapter 14

Finding joy in the ruins

In the months following Bob's death I was on a roller coaster. I felt driven by activity in order to maintain my composure. I sewed for others, joined church committees, did some remodeling to the house, gave away most of Bob's things to those I knew that needed and would appreciate them, worked and socialized with family and friends, and prayed.

I took a plane trip to Phoenix, a car trip to Seattle, and a train ride to Colorado to visit my family. But these things only covered my sorrow. They did not remove it. I baked for church, sewed for hospice and nursing homes, took up collections for the homeless, worked in a soup kitchen and took care of my dog and cat. All this kept my mind busy and helped ease the sadness, until evening came.

Then, tidal waves of sadness and loss would wash over me. I would sit and cry, feeling so empty and lost. I looked into my future and saw nothing. I tried so hard to fill my time with volunteer work so I would feel alive again.

Maybe I was trying to reproduce that awesome feeling I had being with Bob. But here I was alone, trying hard to get motivated, knowing that the one who gave me purpose in life was gone. What was I to do with my life?

Each day I would drive by the cemetery on my way to and from work. I went there to "talk" to Bob weekly in the beginning, but it made me so sad that I started going less often, knowing that I "carried him in my heart forever" anyway. I talked to him regardless of where I was.

I know Bob died because it was his time. God's work through him was finished on earth. But I was still here. I guess there is something I have yet to accomplish. I need to continue to try to carry on the ideas and love Bob left me with. Those things should not die with him. They must be carried forward. I felt I had improved as a person somewhat through these experiences, but just when you think your soul is clean and you've arrived at a place of goodness, imagine a piece of glass you have just cleaned and hold it up to the light. You will still see smudges. That's what the soul is like as you move closer to God. It's always in need of further cleaning.

It reminds me of when I was young, still living in my parent's home. Dad would go to the cupboard to get a glass for a drink of water. He is a precise man. He likes order, cleanliness, and a measure of perfection in many things. I would watch him as he held the clean glass up to the light. He would look at it intently, turning the glass from side to side and then mutter softly, "Well I guess it's clean enough." Mom was right. You are never quite perfect, never finished until you die.

In an effort to help myself move forward, not wanting to be stuck in sadness and self-loathing, I attended a 3-day silent preached retreat. It was a wonderful experience. The topics preached about were directed to women and were about the women of the Bible. Our group of sixty adult ladies were a mix of many races, ages, and backgrounds. But we were all told the same thing. God loves us for who we are and that each individual is loved by Him as though they were the only one in the world. Precious in his sight. He loves me. The ladies in the Bible had a common theme. Before they died and were named Saints each one had a past of imperfection. It was through Faith and through their faults that they learned to follow the right path.

Through this retreat I found the silence to be soothing. It also taught a lot. Although we weren't supposed to speak to each other, as time went on I noticed something wonderful happening. Women would 'talk' with their eyes and body language. A smile and a nod in acknowledgement. Sometimes a simple pat on the arm to say hi or goodbye spoke to me in such a way that I felt an almost painful sense of joyful acceptance. Why don't people smile at each other more? In everyday life I see very few people who talk with their eyes. And yet, the eyes are the window to the soul, it is said.

Bob had such kind eyes. They certainly did reveal his kind soul. Through this experience I find I make more effort to look at people in their eyes when I talk to them. I make a conscious effort to smile because a smile can carry transforming love from the heart which can be transferred from that person to the next and the next. It can change a person's mood and satisfy a sad heart.

In a day when we are so challenged with communication despite the unbelievable many forms of it, can you think of anything more satisfying than someone smiling at you with kind eyes? In this way you are being told, "You matter to me." And the other part of that beautiful image is that the person doing the smiling is also changed. I find myself trying to be nice to others and the amazing affect it has is that it brings me great joy.

So, in silence, I am learning to listen to my conscience (or is that God?). This internal voice tells me that my future is new. A new chapter in my life has begun, inspired by Bob, as well as all the people I have met so far in my life because no one and no experience leaves a person unchanged. Inspired too, by all those good people who stood by Bob and I in prayer and kind acts of many kinds. Through our ordeal I found many believers, many compassionate and gentle souls. As I struggle to move forward into unknown times I bring with me all those I have known, good or bad, who have made me who I am.

And who am I? I am an overachiever who tries too

hard. I am a person with a gambling problem who has wasted time and money for no good reason. I am a person who has been ridiculed and beaten and abandoned by men who were supposed to be those I could trust. I am a person who has been confused, lacking in Faith, driven by pride. I am a person who has looked into a mirror and seen no one. Just a shell of a person beaten by life. And then God sent Bob. My life has been quite a journey.

Bob was one of my crosses. In a good way. The hardships and struggles were part of my healing. My life with Bob taught me the truth. That everyone has pain and disability. Some are visible while others are internal. But everyone hurts. The best way to feel better is to acknowledge you are wounded and stretch out your heart to help others heal. In doing so you find yourself healing as well. The past abuse and abandonment were my healing crosses too.

The people whom I've loved, who refused to love back, taught me about hurt and codependency. The people who physically abused me taught me about emptiness and rejection. Those who emotionally abused me taught me what hatred does. Even my very good childhood had crosses in the form of my sisters' disabilities and the unusual family life we had because of them. The crosses began small and got bigger and bigger until I almost fell beneath them.

And I found the beauty of humanity in those who lovingly stepped up to help me carry that last cross. Co-workers with hearts of gold who listened to me talk and held me up in my sorrow, giving chicken soup and hugs and wonderful emotional support. Family who, although most were far away, were still there to hear me and love me through it. And friends who repeatedly reminded me of my worth. They kept me alive.

I find I am now drawn to those on the fringes. Those people who cannot contribute to society or make money or 'do' anything. People who have been abandoned for dead while still alive. People like that tug at my heart. People like Bob grab at my heart. When I see someone in a wheelchair my heart lunges and I think of him. And I feel it is important now to go forward and tell these people, like I told Brad and Bob, that they matter! Because they are fellow souls, brothers and sisters and an incredibly important part of the journey. And despite what it appears, each person has a very important mission, unique to himself. God makes no mistakes. He has a plan. A plan for each of us to be happy.

I will work continuously to make my soul cleaner. I learn more about myself and my faults as I go. As I deal with one, I find another. But I know that's part of me. There is a purpose for all of it. I still see smudges on the window of my soul. But then, I'm not finished yet!

My grief is no longer buried. I feel it. It is alive within me. I want no sedatives to soften it. No denial so it doesn't hurt. I encourage the feelings I have and know that these are gifts to make me more empathetic, kinder and more understanding. The pain of grief doesn't really leave, but there is peace in acceptance of it. I have found my place. I know I have value. And I will spend the rest of my days praising God because he has done great things for me.

And now, when I look in the mirror and study myself, I see some things I didn't see before. I still see grey hair which no longer holds dye so I've decided grey is fine. I see laugh lines and remember happy times. Truthfully, I kind of see my mother looking back at me. That always makes me smile and remember her love.

I am drawn to what I see in my eyes, my windows to my own soul. In them I see my life in the things I've been witness to. The joy, the hurt, the rejection, the pain, the fear, the love and finally peaceful acceptance that this is me. With all my faults and all my goodness, I am worthy of love and worthy of respect. And I smile contentedly, knowing that no matter what, I am whole in my brokenness. Aware that everything is a gift, I don't have to be in control. I don't have to be perfect. I just need to be me the best way I can. Because God alone suffices. And He is not outdone in generosity.